Pieces and Processes

by Steven Calantropio

A collection of original works, exercises and arrangements
in elemental style with detailed process teaching notes.

SMC 569

SCHOTT

Mainz • London • Madrid • New York • Paris • Prague • Tokyo • Toronto

SMC 569

ISMN   M-60001-043-1
UPC   841886004092
ISBN   1-902455-45-2

Design, typesetting and music engraving by William Holab

This book is dedicated to students of the Cherry Hill Elementary School in River Edge, NJ from 1973–2004. From their talents, interests, and curiosities, I learned how to teach.

Contents

ACKNOWLEDGMENTS

I have used the pieces and processes in this book for many years in my work with both young students and with adults. My first thanks are to the many people who, along this path, have encouraged me to put these ideas into a comprehensible form for publication.

Of the many teachers I have had the pleasure to learn from in my career-long study of Orff Schulwerk, there are two people to whom I wish to offer special thanks. Jane Frazee, former director of the Graduate Programs in Music Education at the University of St. Thomas in St. Paul, Minnesota, has been a teacher, friend and colleague for more than twenty years. We have shared many fine teaching and learning moments together. Professor Richard Gill of Sydney, Australia has also given me the opportunity to see quality elemental music teaching joyfully presented and exceptionally focused on musical skills and concepts.

An opportunity to see Jane or Richard teach should be considered a chance to watch two of the world's finest music teachers in action.

I would also like to thank my significant other, Adele Castaldo, who patiently edits my work and gives me encouragement and support at those times when it is most needed.

Finally, to all of my students young and old who have encouraged me to think long and hard about my Orff Schulwerk teaching, here are some of the results.

—STEVEN CALANTROPIO
SPRING, 2005

1

PREFACE

Pieces and Processes represents some of the work I have done with children during 31 years of teaching in the public school system of River Edge, New Jersey. I spent my entire teaching career from 1973–2004 in that small town and over the years taught music to thousands of suburban youngsters. Along with my studies in Orff Schulwerk, it was the act of everyday instruction that taught me much of what I know about the importance of process teaching. I also learned that a clear understanding of process teaching techniques helps make a better educator.

Clear process teaching has always been the approach to elemental music training, but its domain is not limited to such a narrow area of study. The fact is that *all* good teaching is process oriented. The ability to break down complex concepts into simpler, sequential activities that slowly move towards the desired end is a hallmark of fine teaching in any field.

How does one learn to be a skilled process teacher? I believe that it is accomplished in two ways. First, the individual must have significant experiences learning from teachers who themselves are fine process teachers. If one was lucky, this may have occurred while attending traditional K-12 schooling. One may have experienced excellent instruction as part of the many training opportunities for in-service teachers. Those who attend workshops, conferences, graduate and summer training programs are often exposed to fine teaching.

Secondly, to become a fine process teacher, the individual must have significant experience closely observing a master teacher at work without being involved in the content of the lesson. From a vantage point on the sidelines, he or she can objectively see and evaluate teaching techniques as they are presented without the distractions of being actively involved in the lesson. Apprenticeship and mentoring situations, both formal and informal, provide such opportunities.

In this book I have tried to present clear, effective process techniques that are associated with the elemental music styles of Carl Orff and Gunild Keetman. At the risk of being overly prescriptive, it is my goal to show step-by-step procedures for teaching melodic patterns, rhythmic patterns, harmonic schemes, small structural forms and simple improvisations. While various process techniques are associated with the different lessons, the reader is encouraged to take these processes away from this book and use them in other lessons and classes.

Process teaching techniques work best when they are used to teach repetitive patterns. Music that contains both small and large patterns of melody, rhythm, harmony, and form are easily broken down into smaller teaching units. Not all music lends itself to this kind of deconstruction. The correct choice of songs, instrumental pieces, dances, and exercises is critical to process teaching success. Elemental music, by its very nature, is easily separated into its component elements and parts.

The collected works of composer Carl Orff (1895–1982) and Gunild Keetman (1904–1990) provide examples of just such music. These pattern-based works form the core of what is collectively known as Orff Schulwerk. Both Orff and Keetman used the term *elemental music* in describing their work. The term implies a genre of music that is drawn from the basic elements of rhythm, melody, harmony, and form. It is music stripped of intellectual complexities, closely related to speech and movement, and draws its inspirations from those human impulses that are common to all people.

It is not the purpose of this book to explore the intricacies of elemental style in detail. Readers are encouraged to receive further training in Orff Schulwerk through the many workshops, conferences, and summer courses that are presented for this purpose. The American Orff-Schulwerk Association is a national organization whose goal is to foster the understanding and spread of Carl Orff and Gunild Keetman's work. They provide directories of training venues throughout the country as well as lists of teachers who have proven expertise in the approach.

American Orff-Schulwerk Association
PO Box 391089
Cleveland, OH 44139–808
(440) 543–5366
www.aosa.org

INTRODUCTION

In its simplest form, *Pieces and Processes* is a collection of original works and arrangements that draw upon the elemental compositional styles of Orff and Keetman as inspiration. The works included in *Pieces and Processes* represent some of my efforts to create a collection of new works that are composed or arranged according to elemental music concepts found in the Orff Schulwerk. Some are pieces meant for performance situations, a few are arrangements of folk material and some are teaching exercises rather than performance pieces. They are sequenced to correspond with the organization of *Music for Children*, the five volumes that comprise the basic teaching materials of Orff Schulwerk. This is a harmonic and melodic organizational scheme which starts with pentatonic idioms and moves through drone accompanied scales and modes, nonfunctional triads ending with functional harmony. While this collection does not include examples that illustrate all of the Orff-Keetman models, the pieces are loosely organized along these lines.

A renewed interest in the elemental style of Orff and Keetman has led to a fresh look at the compositional approaches they employed. The original works were well crafted musical miniatures that lent themselves to further elaboration and improvisation. The excitement these pieces still create among children and adults who experience them suggests that a regeneration of that compositional style is appropriate.

It will be clear to the reader who examines these materials that this is not a primer of elemental style. Teachers will need previous experiences working in this style before presenting the materials to their students. Success in presenting these lessons will depend on:

- the study and assimilation of the process steps in the lesson prior to presenting them to students.
- a familiarity with elemental musical media and the ability to express oneself musically in each. These include speech, body percussion, unpitched and barred percussion, recorder, and movement.
- a singing voice that is accurate in pitch with a pleasing tone quality.
- a sense of students' readiness to assimilate the musical content of a lesson. It is not a case of what grade a specific lesson is designed for. Rather, student readiness will depend on the actual knowledge and experience gained through past training and instruction.

Prerequisites to student success and enjoyment of these lessons include:

- the ability to hear, remember, repeat, and adapt patterns of rhythm, melody, and harmony
- significant experience and reasonable technique in elemental media

- a reasonably accurate singing voice
- the ability to move freely in an unselfconscious manner when called for in the course of a lesson

Along with this collection of original works, I have made an attempt to begin to codify some of the process teaching techniques that are used in quality elemental music teaching. We know that in her work with children during the initial stages of Schulwerk development, Gunild Keetman modeled fine teaching process as an integral part of the lesson. Along with the quality materials she created, Keetman left us the legacy of organized process teaching. It has become part of our educational tradition.

I feel I must include a thought or two on the use of musical notation in the process teaching suggestions found in this book. Orff and Keetman said little about the teaching of music reading and writing in their written works. While the function of music reading is not part of the truest elemental traditions found in world music and folk idioms, contemporary students' dependency on visual materials oblige us to include it as a cornerstone of modern music education. Notation skills should be developed concurrently with elemental music skills which are not dependent upon note reading. Therefore lessons may include brief examples of standard musical notation with the understanding that elemental traditions are essentially aural and kinesthetic, not visual in nature.

Regardless of whether or not the reader chooses to teach a particular selection from the book, he or she can benefit from reading through the teaching process associated with the selection. The techniques presented adapt to many different situations and create a readily available toolbox from which one can find ways to teach musical concepts or ideas. While no one of them is sufficient by itself, a combination of techniques will bring elemental music to life for teacher and students.

HOW TO USE THIS BOOK

Take some time to look over the pieces in this book. When you have decided which piece to teach, consider the following suggestions:

1. Before presenting any materials to students, be sure to familiarize yourself with the musical content of the selection. Play the parts on the indicated instruments if possible, sing the melodies, clap the rhythms, and perform the body movements or dance steps until you are familiar with all elements of the lesson. Note any particular concerns such as vocal problems, mallet technique, or movement challenges directly on the score. It is likely that your students may have the same problems.

2. Read through the process steps noting where you may need to add additional instructions for students.

3. Identify and prepare any visual materials you may need for the lesson presentation. These can be charts, visual diagrams, overhead projections, notated rhythmic and melodic patterns, or structure diagrams. Keep the visual materials direct and uncluttered.

4. Take only a few small steps in each lesson, reviewing the previously learned material before adding to it. The majority of these experiences will take multiple lessons to learn. Have fun with the presentation, challenging your students to make progress with you. Mix the learning of these pieces with other classroom activities.

5. The lessons in this volume are convergent in nature; that is, they start out with a distinct product or piece as a finishing point. The experience should not end there. Use the completed pieces as starting points for divergent thinking. Change the meter, tonality, improvise over the accompaniment, create new accompaniments, use the text in a different way; the possibilities will grow as the students' and teacher's creative spirits grow. Here the Schulwerk offers its greatest challenge and its greatest reward; to play with the music as well as to play it!

You may choose to use *Pieces and Processes* only as a teaching reference. If so, try reading through the process steps of each lesson with an understanding of why each step is taken, what comes before and after it. This is certainly only a small sampling of what actually is involved in creative Schulwerk teaching. Note new or interesting techniques that you see in your professional training directly into the book. Make this volume a living source book by adding your own lessons, comments, observations, and cross references. Tape them directly onto the pages, write in the margins, photocopy and reduce relevant materials, to specifically fit the book.

Most of all, learn to see process in all of your life's work. That is what truly makes the journey as important as the destination!

A PROCESS TEACHING TOOL BOX

The following collection represents some of the tools that fill a teaching tool box. They are the process techniques used in teaching the elements of melody, rhythm, and harmony in these lessons. Each tool contains a reference to a piece that illustrates its use. The collection of such tools is just a start. As is the case with any craftsperson, the teacher must learn which tool is the best for the job.

Melody

- **Isolate melodic configurations** (7. Brian Boru's March)
  I define *melodic configurations* as melodic patterns notated as a series of whole notes stripped of any unnecessary visual elements (stems, flags, filled note heads, extra staff lines). The whole notes imply no time or absolute pitch value, only melodic curve. They should be seen as transportable motives that can be moved to many starting points. For consistency, each melodic configuration begins on a line. When using melodic configurations, first ask students to describe the number of notes in the pattern, how it moves by step, skip, or repeat and the absolute pitch names of the pattern if it were to begin on a specific starting note. Then, after identifying a specific starting pitch, use a technique which I have termed *snapping through* the pattern, where each consecutive note is played, sung, or sounded in response to an exaggerated finger snap of the teacher (**A**; *below*). In this way, the teacher carefully observes student responses and corrects problems before they become habitual. The finger snapping eventually is performed in rhythm with the students now echoing the pattern in rhythm (**B**). They then visually observe the pattern notated correctly, if the lesson requires this step. (**C**).

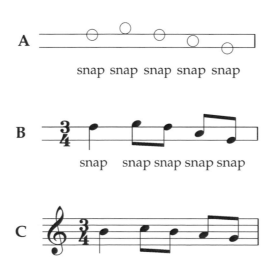

- **Echo** (4. 7/8 Dance)
  The simple act of echoing patterns played or sung by the teacher is also the easiest way to learn melodic and rhythmic patterns. The echo response is the foundation for learning in childhood and it occupies the same important position in elemental music teaching.

- **Use a melodic skeleton** (10. Simi Yadech)
  Identify the pitches that establish the skeleton or framework of a melodic pattern. They usually occur on the strong beats of the measure. Present them first in whole note notation. Slowly add the missing notes which are usually ornaments of the skeletal pitches.

- **Antiphony** (9. 10/8 Dance)
  After dividing the melody into phrases or motives, the students answer a motive played or sung by the teacher. Keep repeated motives in student parts at first. Later, students and teachers change parts. Then ask students to perform both parts in sequence.

- **Manipulate melodic motives** (8. Decorated Third Exercise)
  Thinking of melodic motives as pieces in a puzzle, present new patterns as manipulations of older ones. Try inversions, retrograde (reverse), octave or other interval transposition, changes in metrical elements, removing or adding pitches, dovetailing or conjoining two separate elements.

- **Relate to known melodies** (6. Phrygian Melody)
  Sometimes a new melody will have a melodic curve similar to another well known tune. Relate the new melody to the old and then slowly adapt it.

- **Teach melody cumulatively** (10. Simi Yadech)
  Try slowly teaching a melody in cumulative fashion, adding one or more pitches to the end of a pattern and allowing students to discover the new notes.

- **Fragment and teach** (2. Canon for Xylophones)
  Fragment a melody into parts that have some element in common such as phrase lengths, tone sets, melodic curve, or interval pattern. Teach the melody, assembling it fragment by fragment. Reconstructing it in this way can help students learn a longer example.

- **Use graphics** (1. Little Bitty Man)
  Dictate melodic patterns from visual representations of the scale. Such pitch representations can use sol-fa names, scale degree numbers, or absolute pitch letter names and can be in the shape of ladders, staircases, bars on an instrument, or any other appropriate and uncluttered imagery.

- **Relate to body percussion** (11. Jeremiah)
  The four traditional levels of body percussion are step, pat, clap, snap. These also imply melodic pitches by their timbre and vertical spacing. They can be

used to teach simple melodic patterns by translating each body percussion timbre into a pitch equivalent.

- **Identify and use melodic sequences** (10. Simi Yadech)
  Melodic sequences are often found in elemental music. Once children can identify sequences, they can use them to assemble longer melodic patterns.

Rhythm

- **Relate to speech** (1. Little Bitty Man)
  One of the foundations of elemental music is the teaching of rhythmic patterns using speech equivalents. Find appropriate words, phrases, sentences, rhymes, and proverbs to teach rhythm patterns.

- **Relate to directive speech** (7. Brian Boru's March)
  Choose a text to teach a rhythm pattern that not only conveys the desired rhythmic flow but gives the individual specific playing directions through the chosen text.

- **Augment and diminish** (1. Little Bitty Man)
  Children can understand the idea of twice as fast or half as fast. In some cases, teaching a rhythm at a particular speed and then augmenting or diminishing it clarifies the structure of the rhythm.

- **Relate to known rhythm** (7. Brian Boru's March)
  As is the case with melodies, sometimes a new rhythmic pattern is similar to one experienced in a familiar rhyme or poem. Start with the known rhythm and then adapt it into the new example.

- **Relate to movement** (9. 10/8 Dance)
  Relate rhythmic or metric patterns to previously learned locomotor movements.

- **Morph rhythms** (1. Little Bitty Man)
  Start with a simple version of a rhythm and then "morph" it slowly, substituting notes with rests, subdividing beats, and tying notes together.

- **Distribute rhythms** (5. Betty Botter)
  Draw multiple smaller rhythmic motives out of a longer rhythmic pattern.

- **Rhythmic antiphony** (9. 10/8 Dance)
  Divide complex rhythmic and metric patterns into parts with the teacher performing one part and students the other. Eventually, change parts and then have students perform the whole rhythm.

- **Fill rests** (3. Lullaby)
  Use sounds, words, or gestures to fill up rests when teaching a rhythm pattern, eventually substituting silence for the added sound.

Harmony

- **Use body percussion** (7. Brian Boru's March)
  Dictate harmonic changes with body percussion patterns. Each different harmony is assigned to a particular body percussion timbre.

- **Isolate chord roots** (12. Sing Hallelujah)
  Isolate and diagram chord roots in visual form. Use boxes or staff notation with Roman numerals or chord letter names. Ask students to sing and play chord roots first without rhythm, then in time.

- **Hand patterns** (9. 10/8 Dance)
  Use creative hand patterns with partners to show harmonic changes. Any activity done in partner format requires *both* participants to know the changes. The learned teach the unlearned!

Pieces and Processes

1. Little Bitty Man

Southern Field Song
arranged by Steven Calantropio

The melody of this simple field song uses four of the five *pentatonic* pitches. Correct out of tune singing as the descending intervals in the tune can pull weaker singers flat.

1. Begin the lesson by singing the four three-note patterns below, asking the children to repeat the third note you have sung two more times. In such melodic exercises, a visual tone ladder of sol-fa names, letters, or scale degree numbers can be used for reinforcement.

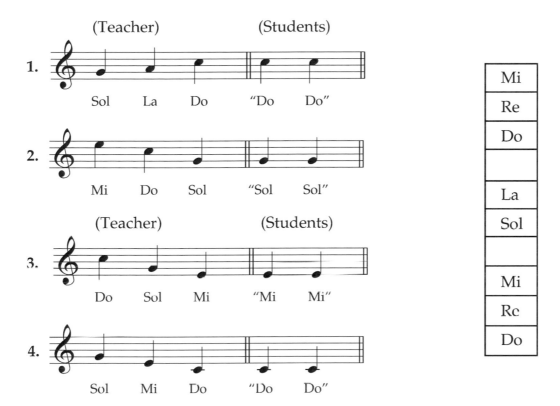

Mi
Re
Do
La
Sol
Mi
Re
Do

Ask children to substitute the word "Lord" for each of the two notes that they sing while you sing the actual text of verse one. Change parts with the children and then ask them to sing the whole melody with you.

Verse 2 : "pickin' up sand, Lord, Lord"
Verse 3 : "grain by grain, Lord, Lord"

2. Teach the bass metallophone part by beginning with a little chant:

One for a nick- el, two for a dime.

Ask students to perform the rhythm, patting it on their right knee while patting a pulse on the left knee:

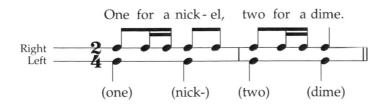

When this is comfortable, explain the principle of *augmentation* to the students, telling them that each note value is now doubled in value and the pattern is played half as fast. Transfer this slow rhythm to the bass metallophone playing the tones of the bordun (C–G); move the G to A on the text **"for a"** and "nick-**EL**."

3. The glockenspiel line is taught rhythmically first. Start with rhythm 1 (below) on the chalk board, slowly erasing notes and adding rests and ties. Ask the children to clap each new variation several times as an ostinato before moving to the next change. When the final rhythm is secure, students slowly add the pitches. This can be done in cumulative fashion; the teacher claps the whole pattern in rhythm, singing only the first two notes (E–G). Students play back only the sung notes. Add the next two pitches and finally another three. Students should play only the sung pitches, adding new ones when the first are secure.

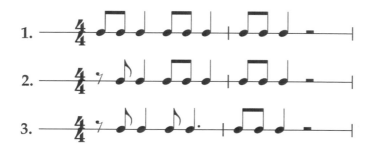

4. The finger cymbal and alto metallophone parts can be layered onto the bass metallophone part from body percussion cues given by the teacher and linked to the text. The alto metallophone plays on the second "Lord"; finger cymbals sound on the first and third (**LIT**-tle bitty **MAN**).

For performance, ask students to sing a fourth verse using the text of the first verse but now sung as a four part canon at the interval of two beats. Eliminate all instrumentation except the bass metallophone which plays a tremolo on low C.

Little Bitty Man
Verse 4: Canon

2. Canon for Xylophones

Steven Calantropio

Allegro

This canon for alto and bass xylophones is based on a tonic pitch of *mi* (E) in the standard pentatonic tone set. In my opinion, *mi* pentatonic is the most exotic sounding of the pentatonic realms. The absence of a perfect fifth above the tonic pitch challenges the composer to create the sense of *mi* as a tonal center. When performed in canon, interest is created by the contrast of ascending and descending melodic contours between leading and following parts.

1. An analysis of the melody shows that it is in a strict **A-A-B/B-A** form. Students can quickly learn the **B** section by finding word equivalents for the following two rhythms:

Tex - as   Min - ne - so - ta

Ask students to speak and clap the rhythms in succession and then in reverse to create a longer pattern:

Tex - as, Min-ne - so - ta,   Min-ne - so - ta, Tex - as

Next eliminate the circled syllables, clapping and repeating the altered pattern:

Moving to the xylophones with F and B bars removed, direct students to begin on the high E bar with the right hand and play this rhythm, alternating mallets, descending bar by bar until the low E is reached. At this point they ascend to the high E bar and repeat the whole pattern again.

2. The A section of the canon can be learned by dividing it into three distinct melodic elements.

1.

       L R L R L R L R   L R L R

Teach pattern 1 through alternate hand-thigh patting. Transfer it to instruments with appropriate pitches.

R. Knee
L. Knee

2.

       L R L R   L R L R L R L R

The "running" pattern of eighth notes begins with the left hand and moves to the lowest bar of the instrument before returning to the high E.

3.

       L   R   L   R   L   R   L

This pattern begins with the left hand which crosses over the right hand on the circled pitches.

When the patterns are secure, connect them together to create the **A** section. Remembering the **A-A-B/B-A** form, students should be able to play through the complete melody at first slowly, then in a quick tempo. The canon is best performed first in unison and then with the alto xylophones leading; bass xylophones enter after one measure.

3. Lullaby

Steven Calantropio

This gentle melody moves in a slow 6 meter and is built around the I–ii harmonic progression over a tonic pedal. The voice part is limited to the *pentachord* in F major. A spare musical texture allows the voice to predominate.

1. Direct students to set up barred instruments in F major. Using a visual representation of the scale in a tone ladder orientation, the students can observe and then imitate the patterns below that you outline by touching the visual diagram. Slowly adapt the patterns as noted in the steps below until the actual glockenspiel countermelody is developed.

This pattern is presented for echo slowly without rhythm. Students observe the descending scale pattern and that *sol* is played twice.

The same pitch patterns are now presented in a slow 6/8 meter.

The eighth-note elaboration in the third bar is added. Ask students to repeat the entire melody.

The connector is added in the first ending along with the upward leap and cadence of the second ending.

Ask the glockenspiel players to practice their line against a slow pulse played on F on the bass metallophone. Then add the bass metallophone rhythm as scored.

2. The alto metallophone part and the finger cymbal can be prepared simultaneously. Instruct students to imitate the following body percussion pattern as the bass metallophone provides the pedal accompaniment:

Students playing the alto metallophone now play G–F alternating with D–F on the hand claps. Finger cymbals play on the finger snaps. There is no sound associated with the thigh patting gesture.

The limited range of the melody allows for easy teaching. Use the **A-B-A-B1** nature of the melodic phrases as a starting point. Divide the melody into two-bar phrases, asking students to sing the repetitive **A** phrase while you add the **B** and **B1** phrases. Change parts when secure; then combine into the complete melody.

A final performance arrangement of the *Lullaby* treats the bass metallophone, alto metallophone, and finger cymbal patterns as introduction and accompaniment to the first verse. Continue the instrumental parts without singing, adding the glockenspiel countermelody as an interlude. End with the singing of the second verse with all parts, including glockenspiels. A simple coda of the melody, hummed with accompaniment parts, brings the piece to a close.

You may wish to use the *Lullaby* as a vocal piece at some point, sung without accompaniment. In this case, use the vocal arrangement on p. 21, drawn from patterns similar to the instrumental accompaniment.

Lull - a - by, lull - a - by, An- gels, their watch o'er you keep - ing____

Lull - a - by, lull - a - by, An - gels are keep-ing, sing____

'by, sing lull - a - by, Lull - a - by. Sing lull - a - by.

Lull - a - by, lull - a - by, while you lie peace-ful - ly sleep - ing.____

Lull - a - by, lull - a - by, while you sleep.

'by, sing lull-a - by lull - a - by sing lull - a - by.

4. 7/8 Dance

Steven Calantropio

7/8 Dance

This moving drone accompanied rhythmic dance in 7/8 time shows the development of the ii triad through the convergence of the accompaniment and melody patterns. The melody itself is limited to the G major pentachord.

Jen - ni - fer   Bob - by

1. With the teacher at a set of bongo, timpani, conga drums or any percussion instrument with a high-low contrast, students move about open space. Play groups of three eighth notes, associating the rhythm with the name **Jen-ni-fer** or any three syllable name where the stress falls on the first syllable. Challenge students to step forward on the first syllable and clap the second and third. Then change to groups of two eighth notes with a name such as **Bob-by** where students step on the first syllable and clap the second. After a period of warm-up, move directly into a repeated pattern of 7/8:

Jen - ni - fer Bob-by Bob-by

Students with partners experiment with ways to show the articulation of the strong and weak notes in each grouping. For example, they can step on the strong first eighth note and clap partner's hands for the second and third.

2. After the basic metrical grouping 3+2+2 has been explored, show students the following patterns below that constitute the rhythmic vocabulary of the entire lesson. Explain that tying two or three eighth notes together produces longer note values. The groupings can also be substituted with equal rest values. Ask them to chant and clap the patterns while you accompany with a constant eighth note pulse. They can improvise others if they wish.

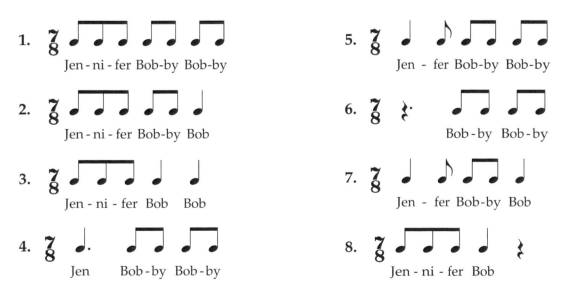

1. Jen - ni - fer Bob-by Bob-by
2. Jen - ni - fer Bob-by Bob
3. Jen - ni - fer Bob   Bob
4. Jen   Bob - by Bob - by

5. Jen - fer Bob-by Bob-by
6. Bob - by   Bob - by
7. Jen - fer Bob-by Bob
8. Jen - ni - fer Bob

3. Prepare the bass xylophone ostinato by asking students to pat both knees with both hands for two measures using rhythm 1. Begin to move the right hand to the outside, top and inside of the right thigh following the direction of the upper voice of the moving bordun, while keeping the left hand stationary.

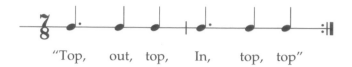

"Top,   out,   top,   In,   top,   top"

Speak the directive text for right hand placement in rhythm and, when secure, transfer to the bass xylophone as scored. This pattern continues throughout. The alto xylophone part can be prepared from rhythm #5. Ask the bass and alto xylophone players to practice their parts together.

4. Help students to recognize that the melody is limited to the pentachord or first five notes of the G scale. Using the rhythm patterns already established, invite the class to listen to and echo improvised melodic contours, eventually leading them to the rhythms and contour that are part of the melody. Some possibilities are:

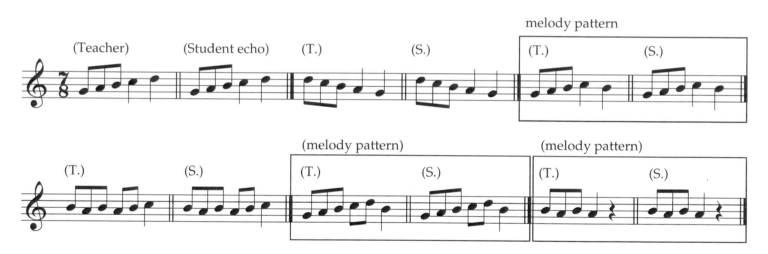

5. The two-bar soprano xylophone ostinato can be approached from rhythm #6. Instruct students to clap it first over the playing of the bass xylophone and alto xylophone pattern. Then transfer the pattern to the instruments. The glockenspiel can be added to the start of each bar of the **B** section. On the return to the **A** section of the piece, a few experienced recorder players can parallel the melody a third above, applying an elemental music technique termed *paraphony*.

6. The uneven long-short-short beats of 7/8 meter lead naturally to movement. Students can experiment with dance patterns using the bass xylophone rhythm as the basis for their creations.

5. Betty Botter

Betty Botter bought some (butter) "But," she said, "this butter's (bitter.)

If I put it in my (batter,) it will make my batter (bitter.)

But a bit of (better butter) will but make my batter (better.")

So, she bought some better butter, (put it in her bitter batter)

AND IT MADE HER BATTER BETTER!

So 'twas better (Betty Botter) bought a bit of (better butter.)

This playful tongue twister demonstrates a technique called *distributed rhythm* where a single, extended rhythm pattern is distributed into smaller motives for multiple players. In any speech exercise, remember to keep the speech light and playful, accenting the musical qualities of pitch, color, duration, and emotional content of the text.

1. Displaying the diagram above, students follow the text as the teacher reads it without pulse. The indented line is emphasized dynamically and with a *cesura* (pause) before continuing *a tempo*. Divide the text into lines, phrases, and words while continuing to explore the possibilities of large group, small group, solo, and antiphonal speech effects.

2. When students demonstrate a command of the text, perform the entire exercise while accompanying the speaking with a four-beat body percussion pattern.

The text should move in strict eighth notes, with *rubato* tempo during the indented line, continuing *a tempo* for the last line. Try alternating lines and phrases between teacher and students, or among groups of students.

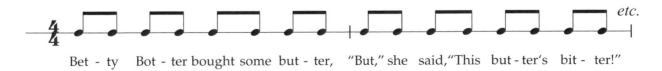

Bet - ty   Bot - ter bought some but - ter,   "But," she said, "This but - ter's   bit - ter!"

3. Now ask the class to observe the boxed, circled, and underlined elements of the text. Their task at first is to speak only the boxed words while the teacher speaks the entire text in rhythm. The isolated boxed motive should be inflected and

musical. Everyone speaks the entire indented line. Next, try the circled text only, then the underlined words or parts of words. Divide the class into three groups and assign each group to box, circle, or underline while the instructor performs all of the words. Now, each assigned group speaks the boxed, circled, and underlined words while silently thinking the entire poem. All speak the indented line as before.

4. A few students from each group can now transfer their rhythms to unpitched percussion instruments. Wood instruments play the boxed words, idiophones (rattles, cabasa, guiro) play the circled words, and underlined words are played on metal instruments. All play the indented line. Replace the entire text with a repeated eighth note pulse on the low C of the bass xylophone that accompanies the unpitched instrument patterns, moving to the pitch G on the indented line and then returning to C until completed.

Bet - ty Bot - ter bought some but- ter...   AND IT MADE HER BAT- TER BET- TER!

5. You may wish to develop other pitched accompaniment patterns to add to the texture. They should be played along with the bass xylophone, playing the indented line in unison on G and then returning to the pattern. Children enjoy the exciting texture of the whole experience, which has now moved from a speech exercise to an instrumental one.

6. Phrygian Melody

Steven Calantropio

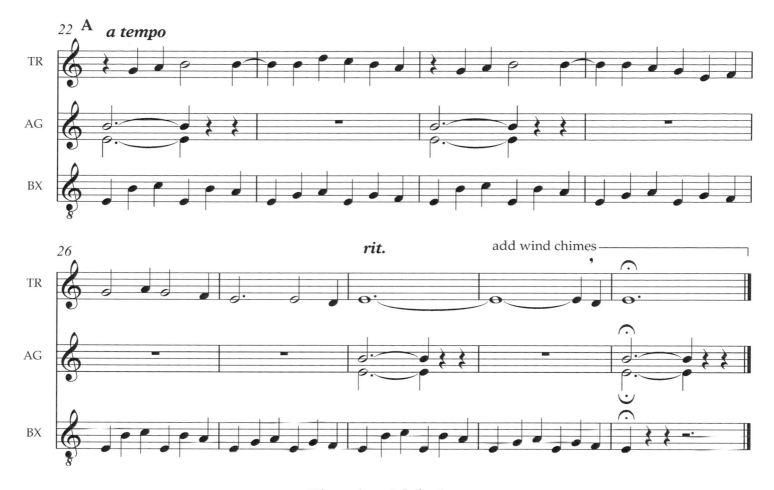

Phrygian Melody

This work in the Phrygian mode is accompanied by a tonic drone and demonstrates the close harmonic connection between the melody and the accompanying ostinato. The Phrygian mode, limited to only perfect and minor intervals, conveys the melancholy, brooding tones of late autumn or early winter. With such expressive content, the piece has been a good choice for winter concerts. Solo choreography or a group dance adds to the performance. The instrumentation indicated within parenthesis is also a possibility, placing the arrangement an octave higher than the given instrumentation.

1. In learning the first theme in this arrangement, lead the students to make a connection with the familiar children's melody *London Bridge*. After reviewing the tune, isolate the first phrase of the melody:

Now, introduce a new version of the phrase:

Ask students to remember this pattern as it will return later in the lesson. Continue by explaining that 6/4 time is counted in six and felt as two groups of three beats. Ask students to count aloud and then clap, observing the metrical accent on beats one and four :

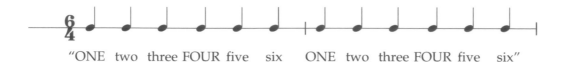

"ONE two three FOUR five   six   ONE two three FOUR five   six"

Next, have the students eliminate the first beat of a two measure pattern, thinking and feeling the missing beat while counting:

"ONE two three FOUR five   six   ONE two three FOUR five   six"

By this point, they should be able to count silently while clapping only. Add the following ties:

The first tie can be notated as a half note:

With this two-bar rhythm pattern written out twice, call the students' attention to the following:

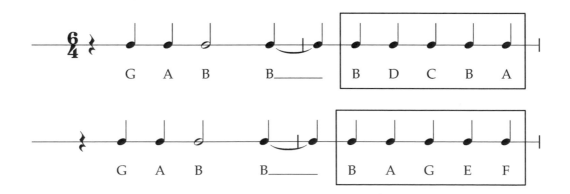

Students play the unboxed part of the melody on recorders while the teacher plays the boxed pitches. When secure, change roles with students, having them play the boxed areas. Combine these elements to play the whole pattern. Now ask students to recall the new version of *London Bridge* that they learned earlier and attach it to what they have just learned. The **A** section melody of the piece is complete:

(in 6)

TR

5

2. Counting in 6 is now becoming more familiar to students who can begin to learn the first accompanying ostinato. Begin with the sound of a broken drone based on the tonic and dominant pitches E–B. Using the indicated mallet alternation, have students articulate the drone in 6/4.

L   R   R   L   R   R

Explain that the upper pitch of the drone can lead to an upper neighbor or to a lower neighbor. Let them explore this movement by playing the pattern:

L   R   R   L   R   R

The same movement can be applied to the third above the tonic pitch:

L   R   R   L   R   R

Combining the two patterns creates the ostinato:

L   R   R   L   R   R   L   R   R   L   R   R

3. Prepare the B section ostinato with the following body percussion pattern:

Snap
Clap
Pat

L   R   R

31

While the class performs this ostinato, transfer the two finger snaps to a broken octave E (low/high) on the bass xylophone. Transfer the thigh patting to a low F, played with the right hand. The two claps are left silent resulting in the accompaniment figure:

4. Discuss the concept of *trichords* with the students. These are three note patterns that move in an ascending or descending stepwise motion from the starting pitch. Invite students to echo the six trichord patterns below, notated without rhythmic value:

As students become comfortable with the trichord recorder fingerings, begin to play them as quarter note fragments of 6/4 meter. Now gradually alter these patterns.

- Repeat the last note of pattern 1 rhythmically adapting the two Ds as scored.
- Tie the last note of pattern 3 and the first note of pattern 4.
- Follow pattern 6 with another B.

At this point, show students the notated melody of the **B** section. Circle the adapted trichord patterns on the score. Ask them to analyze the remainder of the melody circling other trichord patterns which may be also be elongated with an extra repeated pitch as they discovered in pattern 1. The whole **B** section ends with a descending pair of trichords played in half notes, creating a two-bar hemiola that leads back to the **A** theme.

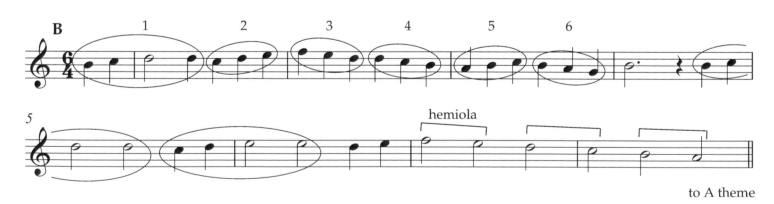

to A theme

6. The glockenspiel part is easily established through finger snaps on the missing first beat of the **A** melody in measures 5 and 7, and along with the melody in measure 11. The part is also played in the corresponding measures of the **A** section when it returns. Adding a slow glissando on the wind chimes brings the piece to a pensive ending.

7. Brian Boru's March

Traditional Irish Melody
arranged by Steven Calantropio

D.C. al Fine

7. Brian Boru's March

Older children enjoy learning this traditional Irish folk melody. Its haunting modal quality captivates both performers and listeners.

The teaching techniques presented for *Brian Boru's March* will challenge students' abilities in elemental process teaching and learning styles. Their ability to hear, remember, and adapt extended rhythmic, harmonic, and melodic patterns is essential before attempting to teach this work. It is assumed that students who would be learning this particular arrangement would have some skill at interpreting standard musical notation because notated visual aids will assist the learning process. As with any sustained learning experience, the March should be approached over a period of multiple lessons and exposures.

Children express curiosity concerning the title of this melody. Brian Boru, despite the many legends that grew up around him, was an actual historical figure (c. 940–1014 A.D.). After driving invading Norsemen from Ireland, he became the only Irish king to briefly rule over a united Ireland.

1. Students can begin to explore the rhythmic content of this arrangement with a new version of the traditional rhyme *Jack, Be Nimble*. Ask them to speak and clap the rhyme using the traditional 6/8 rhythmic patterns, broken into **A** and **B** phrases.

Traditional

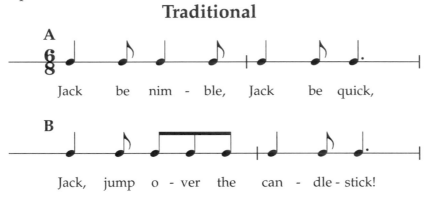

Now create a new version of the rhyme: the first line **A** is repeated three times followed by a new second line which serves to cadence the longer version of the text.

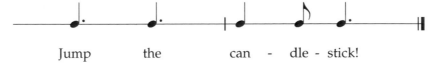

The **B** line is also repeated three times and is again followed by same new cadence line. All clap and speak the new version of the entire rhythm.

New Version

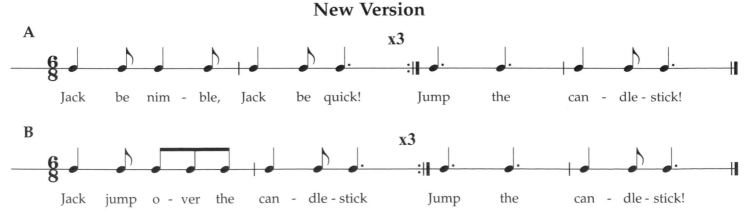

When the new version is secure, students can add locomotor movements that express these compound meter rhythms. These include stepping, skipping, or galloping. Challenge them to create a movement form in small groups that reflects the difference between the **A** and **B** sections as well as the identical cadence of each line.

2. The new version is transferred to the bass xylophone as indicated in the score. Transfer the **A** section by dictating the melodic movement between the notes A and G as a series of clapping (A) and thigh patting (G). The cadence line is adapted to move to low E on the word **the**. For the **B** section of the arrangement, dictate the low C pitch from a seated position, tapping the floor lightly on the first repetition; the remaining pitches and the cadential ending can be presented as above with clapping and patting. As always, speaking the words aloud and then thinking them silently will assist in learning the part.

3. The alto xylophone part is prepared through speech and body percussion. Using alternating hands, ask students to pat the triplet rhythm of the word **straw-ber-ry** two times on the left thigh starting with the left hand. Substitute the text **Get ME a strawberry** and then repeat the pattern with the words **pick ME a strawberry.** Now, move the right hand to the right thigh only on the word **ME.** This rhythmic pattern is repeated three times and cadences by substituting the last **pick ME a strawberry** with the text **right from the top** where the sweetest strawberries are usually found! Transfer the pattern to octave E pitches on the instrument. When the pattern is secure, ask the students to lower the second repetition of the pattern one bar to octave D, returning to the original pitch for the third repetition and cadential ending. See below:

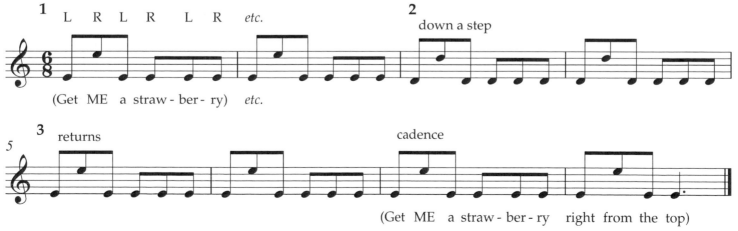

The **B** section of the alto xylophone part can be taught using directive speech. Students identify and move their mallets through three pairs of pitches.

When they can move comfortably from one pair to the next, use the directive speech pattern "**play them together, together and stop!**" This directs students to play the pitches harmonically in the rhythm of the words. The pattern is played once for each pair of pitches, finishing with the cadential pattern from the **A** section.

4. The **A** section of alto glockenspiel part can be taught directly at the instrument. Ask students to observe, describe, and play this simple melodic configuration:

Students should understand that the pattern can be played from many starting pitches on their instruments. With no specific rhythm, play it starting on the pitch A, then move it up one bar to B and again to C, creating a melodic *sequence*. Clapping two pulses in rhythm, students answer your gesture by playing the sequence they have learned, now performed in rhythm. End with three final finger snaps which eventually are substituted with octaves E, G and A.

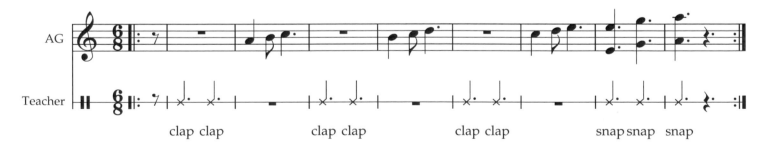

Now clapping only once, sing the entire glockenspiel melody including the pickup notes to each phrase. Ask students to identify the pitch of the added pickup note and add it to their part. Students learn the **B** section of the glockenspiel melody by listening to the alto xylophone part and playing on the cue word **Stop** when it occurs in the directive text. They play octave Gs twice and As once before cadencing as in the **A** section.

"Stop"   "Stop"   "Stop"

MELODY

A section

The sequential nature of the recorder melody makes it fairly easy to teach. Start with the three melodic motives below:

A Section

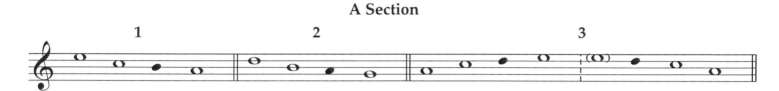

Play through each motive at first without rhythmic value, omitting the darkened pitch. Students identify the obvious triads that are formed. Note that the first four notes of pattern 3 reverse themselves for the second half of the motive. Slowly extend and adapt the **A** melody motives by adding the darkened *passing tone* pitch and repeating the last pitch in each. Play pattern 1 twice, pattern 2 twice, pattern 1 twice again, then pattern 3 once leaving out the high E in parenthesis and repeating the final pitch 2 more times. The rhythm of the melody can now be added; it is quite repetitious. The following diagram will help students memorize the melody.

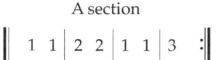

A section

‖ 1 1 | 2 2 | 1 1 | 3 :‖

B Section

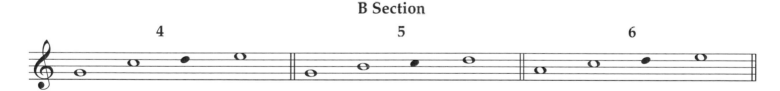

B Section

Play through the motives of the B section, leaving out the darkened pitch as before and pointing out the triads formed by each pattern. Now add in the darkened passing tone. The melodic motives of the **B** section patterns are extended by rocking between the last pitch and the third pitch of the pattern twice. Pattern 5 rocks between the last and second pitch. In a final adaptation, pattern 6 leaves off the last note. These extended **B** motives cadence with a return to motive 3 played as before.

B section

‖ 4 | 5 | 6 | 3 :‖

A final performance version of *Brian Boru's March* includes an introduction using accompaniment patterns, an improvised hand drum part and a return to the **A** section creating an **A-B-A** form. In traditional performance, the last pitch in patterns 1 and 2 jump an octave in the final **A** section, as on p. 38.

8. Decorated Third Exercise

Steven Calantropio

8. Decorated Third Exercise

The *Orff Schulwerk: Music for Children* volumes contain musical examples that are clearly rooted in historical styles. The decorated third exercises found in *Volume IV: Minor; Drone Bass-Triads* edition of the series are such examples. The colorful, transparent textures of such pieces evoke a sense of music from the Elizabethan era; period composers such as Dowland and Morley wrote lute pieces and songs using these techniques. Modern students also find the colorful sonorities refreshing to the ear.

Teachers may choose to teach the dance that accompanies this exercise first. It is found at the end of the process teaching notes. Hum or sing the melody on a neutral syllable as the students are learning the dance, asking them to join in as they become familiar with the tune.

1. The teaching of the instrumental parts begins with the following melodic motives:

At first ask students to observe the two patterns, discussing the melodic movement in terms of number of pitches, direction, steps or skips. Directing the playing of each consecutive pitch of the melodic motive with an exaggerated finger snap allows the teacher to observe and correct any playing problems. This technique is called *snapping through*: it is described in the Process Teaching Tool Box (page 7). Begin to make the following adaptations:

*   Play motive #1 twice through, leaving a rest at the end of the motive equal to one whole note.
*   Connect this adaptation of motive #1 to motive #2, played as written.
*   Finish with two repetitions of pattern 1 this time inverting the pattern. Start on F and ascend to A with the added rest following the A. When the students are ready, change the snapping to 3/4 meter. The following bass line will result. Now they can play the line with the left hand only.

Ask the students to add a perfect fifth higher to each pitch, played with the right hand. These parallel fifths, while strictly avoided in many musical styles are perfectly acceptable in elemental style and provide a strong harmonic foundation. The moving fifths become the bass metallophone part.

2. Review the construction of traditional triads with the class. Most students can create the third and fifth members of a triad from given root pitches. Explain that the previously learned bass metallophone part uses only the root and fifth of various triads. Ask students to identify and add the missing thirds on their instruments along with the bass metallophone line. In performance, the added thirds should sound one octave above the bass part. You may prefer the lyrical, sustained timbre of the tenor recorder for this step. Performance on alto metallophone, alto xylophone, or tenor recorder that all sound at written pitch will place the thirds in the correct octave above the bass metallophone. Create a sense of cadence by leading the final pitch to the root (A) instead of the third of the last triad.

When this is secure, engage students in a discussion about musical ornaments. Longer notes in a melody can be ornamented; elaborating them creates an engaging melody and gives a sense of melodic movement. While there are many possible ways to ornament a pitch, concentrate on the following five melodic configurations. The black note represents *any* possible starting pitch. Invite students to play the notated ornaments beginning on various exploratory pitches without any specified rhythm:

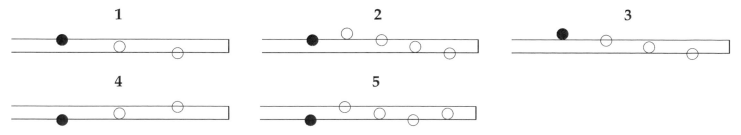

At this point, the teacher may play the first three long note triad thirds in time on recorder or alto metallophone, ornamenting the first two as the actual melody indicates (ornament #1). Ask the students which of the five ornaments, if any, has been applied to each note. Can they imitate those ornaments on their instruments? Continue playing the next three long notes following the same procedure. Proceed, ornamenting two or three long notes at a time, asking students to identify and imitate the models. Finally, add the pickup notes where scored to complete the melody.

3. Add the glockenspiel and finger cymbal parts to the texture by relating them to the moving fifths. They echo the last pattern of fifths played by the bass metallophone, filling the gap created by the measure rest added to both the original and inverted version of pattern 1. Use finger snaps or graphic cues to indicate placement. A simple drone played four times on the bass metallophone along with finger cymbals can serve as an introduction. The following non-traditional dance can also be added to complete the artistic experience.

Dance Directions

Starting position: Dancers with partners in a circle facing center, hands loosely held, open spacing:

Dancers begin with side step R touching L, sidestep L, touching R and then to the R 3 steps RLR bringing L together on last pulse.

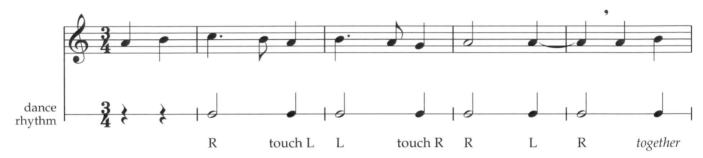

Opposite footwork of above; starting with L and returning to position.

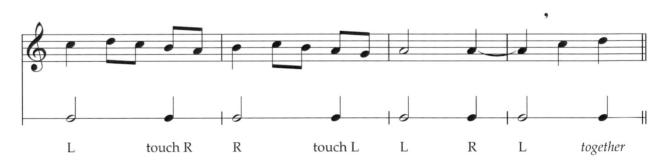

Four steps towards center: RLRL (hands raise as necessary)

Four steps away from center: RLRL; to position: immediately face partner holding R hand against partner's, palm open at face level; L hand on waist.

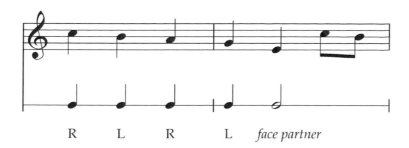

R   L   R   L   *face partner*

Step R to side of partner; touch L; Step L away from partner; touch R. Then partners half circle exchanging positions with four steps.

R   touch L   L   touch R   R   L   R   L   *together*

Exchange hands: L hand now against partner's at face level, R hand at side. Step L to side partner; touch R; Step R away from partner; touch L. Partners then half circle returning to original position with four steps.

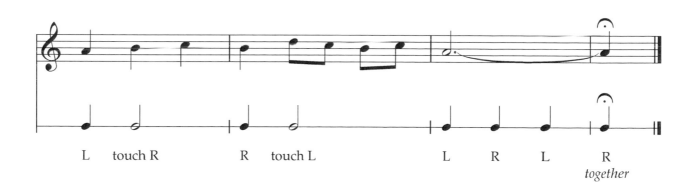

L   touch R   R   touch L   L   R   L   R
                                                     together

As students begin to understand and enjoy this style, challenge them to create improvisations above a different set of moving fifths. The malagueña pattern of descending fifths is often used for this purpose. An important stylistic consideration is that only major and minor triads be used; the diminished triad, which occurs on one scale degree of every key or mode, should never be used in such creations. Its inherent instability excludes its use in elemental music.

9. 10/8 Dance

Steven Calantropio

9. 10/8 Dance

The irregular meter of this playful dance piece naturally stimulates movement and for this reason, movement presents a logical starting point in teaching it. Teachers should note the 2+2+3+3 organization of the meter. It is to be felt as four beats; two short beats consisting of two eighth notes and two long beats consisting of three eighth notes. The speed of the eighth note remains constant within the meter. The **A** section of the tune is five measures long while the **B** section is only four measures, creating tension within the symmetry of the piece.

1. Using hand drum, the teacher plays the following rhythm while students begin to move freely about the open space to the pattern. The instructor and students can speak the text as an aid to movement. (Note: the dotted bar line represents the division between the two short beats and two long beats of the measure.)

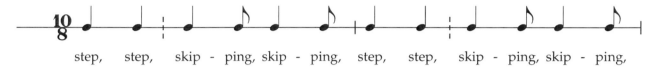

step,   step,   skip - ping, skip - ping, step,   step,   skip - ping, skip - ping,

Students first move to five patterns of the rhythm. The last pattern ends with three steps accompanied by three claps.

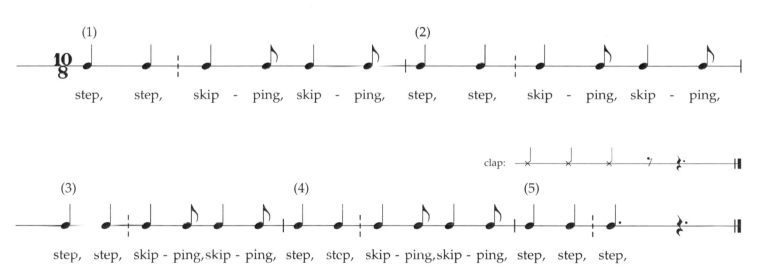

These steps can now be choreographed by students into a dance. Suggest circles, opposing lines, or partners.

2. While a group of students prepare the dance, others transfer the rhythmic pattern to alto xylophones prepared in F major. The first measure is played on the harmonic third F and A. On the second measure, each hand moves out one bar to E and B♭. This movement continues back and forth until the last bar. The final beat is elongated with the text **skip-ping step.**

step   step   skip - ping   step

3. Students now explore the harmonic movement in the work. Each complete measure changes harmony among tonic, subdominant, and dominant triads of F major. After identifying the roots of each of these chords and associating them with the corresponding scale degree numerals, students can sing them based on the diagram.

A section

| I | V⁷ | I | V⁷ | I |

B section

| IV | I | V⁷ | I |

To explore harmonic movement as a group, try the following strategy. Students stand in a double circle facing a partner. While singing the root of the **I** triad without rhythm, partners touch hands. When singing the root of the **IV** triad, each hand moves one position to the right: now each person's left hand touches the left hand of his partner's and the right hand of the person to his partner's left. Return to the original position with the **I** triad; move one position to the left when singing the root of the **V7** triad; now each person's right hand touches his partner's right hand and the left hand of the person to his partner's right. Return to both partner's hands for the **I** triad. The following diagrams visually explain the strategy. Once the harmonic movement is memorized without rhythm, students clap their partner's hands to effect the meter changes; two short and two long beats.

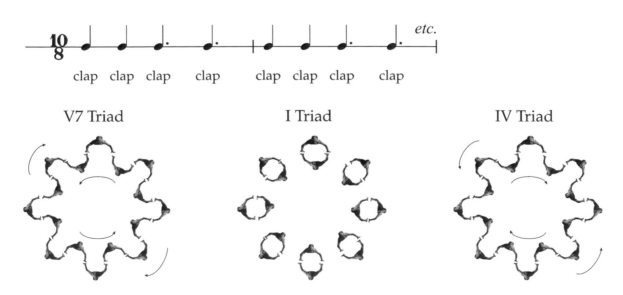

clap clap clap   clap   clap clap clap   clap

V7 Triad   I Triad   IV Triad

4. At this point, students will have discerned the nature of this configuration of 10/8 meter; two short beats precede two long beats. Rhythmically subdividing either the short beats into two eighth notes, the long beats into three eighth notes or by substituting rests for beats creates a number of patterns that will be used in the piece:

(1)   (2)   (3)   (4)

Explore these rhythms by asking one group to clap the short beat rhythms followed by the other clapping the long beat rhythms, exchanging parts when ready. Both groups now clap the complete rhythm. Rhythm 2 is transferred to the bass xylophone. If the students playing the instruments have memorized the harmonic scheme, they should be able to apply rhythm 2 to the harmonic pattern using the tonic, dominant and subdominant triad pitches as scored. Extending the alto xylophone part into the **B** section of the piece is a simple matter of applying the step/skip rhythm of the second process step (pp. 45–46) to the pitches of the subdominant triad.

Use rhythm 3 above to teach the glockenspiel line in the opening section of the piece. The line is a musical sequence starting on the high A and moving down stepwise for each repetition until cadencing on the tonic pitch.

5. The melody of the *10/8 Dance* can be taught slowly at first without rhythm, using melodic motives illustrated on p. 48. Again, an antiphonal dialogue between teacher and students, exchanging parts when secure, clarifies these motives. Students should note the clear sequence of both the teacher and student parts of the motives. After all melodic motives are secure, begin to add rhythm to the patterns. Lastly, invert the teacher portion of pattern 1 and the melody of the **A** section is complete.

The melody of the **B** section can again be taught through notation or by imitation of the teacher's playing. The recorder part is demanding; the B♭ of the key signature will challenge students to play smoothly through the patterns containing that pitch.

Another group of students can continue to choreograph the **B** section using ideas developed earlier in the process, remembering that the three claps at the end of each section are part of the dance.

One performance suggestion may enhance the final result; ask the glockenspiels to delay their entry until the *Da Capo* return to the **A** section of the **A-B-A** form.

An introduction to the piece using the **A** section accompaniment patterns of alto xylophone and bass xylophone establishes the mode and meter of the piece; these patterns, including the glockenspiel line, can also be played as a coda.

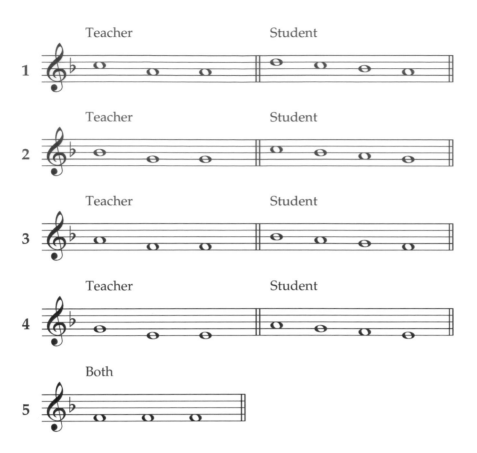

Pattern 1 (inverted)

10. Simi Yadech

Israeli Song
arranged by Steven Calantropio

Si - mi ya-dech   be - ya - di a - ni she-lach, ve - at   she - li.

at she - li.   Hey, hey,   ga-li - yah,___ bat ha - rim yeh fe-fi-yah   fe-fi-yah.

Simi Yadech

This charming Israeli melody uses tonic, subdominant, and dominant chord changes and is easily teachable to children. The arrangement lends itself to dancing as well as singing. Alto recorder players must have intermediate playing skills.

1. Begin by teaching the melody of the **A** section. Some students might play alto recorder reading an octave higher, while the rest of the group sings. Students observe and sight-read melodic pattern 1 with sol–fa or letter names.

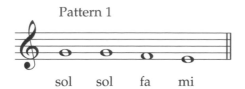

After they have sung the pattern twice, ask them to begin the pattern one note lower, and then one note lower again.

Connect these repetitions without rhythm at first, then with the rhythm of the **A** melody, adding in the circled connector notes.

2. Teach the **B** melody from a notated melodic skeleton. Invite students to read through the pattern without rhythm at first, asking them to sing each pitch using letter names or sol–fa syllables with your finger snaps.

Continue to adapt the pattern adding in repeated tones, passing tones, and finally the melody with rhythm.

Students can now sing the entire melody and, ideally, some can play it on alto recorder. The phonetic pronunciation of the Hebrew text is:

Sih-mee yah day, bay- yah- dee, ah-nee shay-lah, vay-aht shay-lee.
Hay, hay Gah-lee-yah, baht hah-reem yeh feh-fee-yah.

3. While some students play the **A** melody on recorder, others can accompany the tune on the bass xylophone. Ask them to create an ostinato pattern using the pitches C and G and playing them as a broken bordun. As they play their pattern with the recorder melody, challenge them to aurally identify at what point the C ostinato pattern does not seem to fit the melody (measure 3) and explain the need to change to a G and D accompaniment at that point returning to C for the final measure. The harmonic pattern **C – C – G – C (I–I–V–I)** is now established for the **A** section. Calling upon previously learned standard accompaniment patterns, ask students to change the C measures into crossover patterns and play the G measure simply a broken pattern moving to the *alla breve* quarter note pulse. Leave out the last note of the second bar C pattern to allow for mallet position change.

4. Using the same aural approach to finding harmonic changes as encountered in the **A** section, invite students to find the harmonic pattern of the **B** section. The accented A in the sixth bar of the melody becomes a signal for subdominant harmony. With guidance and experimentation, students should arrive at a pattern of **C – F – G – C (I–IV–V–I)**. Adapt the resulting pattern to:

When the movement of mallets from chord to chord is secure, divide the pairs of notes into the following rhythm, adapting the final bar as a first and second ending:

5. The alto xylophone pattern changes between the **A** and **B** sections. In the **A** section, the pattern can be taught from a simple thigh patting rhythm that is transferred to octave G pitches.

For the **B** section, refer back to the harmonic pattern that was discovered by the bass xylophones (**I–IV–V–I**). Alto xylophone players find the E–G harmonic third that fills out the **I** (C) triad, playing it three times. The pattern of harmonic thirds moves up one bar in the second measure, again in the third measure, and opens into a perfect fourth on the last:

6. Another way to teach a melodic pattern is in *cumulative* fashion. Use this approach with the glockenspiel part, singing the first pitch of the melody while the students find it on their instruments. This usually takes some experimentation but provides a valuable ear training exercise as students must hear and remember the pitch, finding it on their instruments without the initial aid of an absolute pitch or sol-fa name. Next, without rhythmic value, sing the first two pitches. Using the sequential number of the pitch sung as text, continue through the pattern. This strategy continues for all eight pitches of the glockenspiel part.

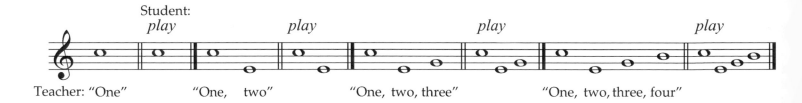

When all eight pitches have been found, sing the rhythm of the glockenspiel part using note numbers. Students should have no trouble applying this rhythm to the melodic pattern already learned.

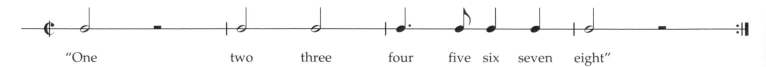

7. The unpitched percussion instrument parts can be taught from body percussion gestures. Ask students to imitate the following body percussion pattern.

When they are secure, claves play only on the clapping gesture which will articulate the scored claves rhythm of the **A** section. The triangle part of the **B** section can be related to the song text. Play on second **HEY** and **GAL- iyah, ha-RIM** and **FE-fi-yah**.

8. An elaborate countermelody such as the soprano recorder line should be learned from notation or through imitation by a few advanced students.

With the orchestration secure, a performance of the arrangement might start with singing of the melody without the soprano recorder. On the second time through, substitute the alto recorder playing melody along with the soprano recorder countermelody. A third repetition brings all parts together with singing. Some simple dance steps can enhance the experience.

Dance Directions

Position: Dancers, without partners, in a circle facing the center, hands loosely held.

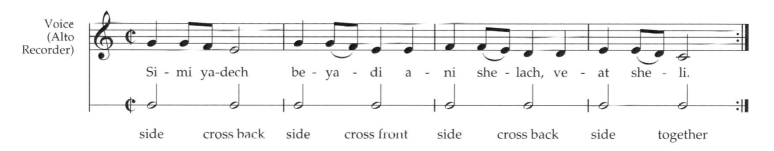

Moving in a half note pulse, dancers grapevine step to the right eight beats, ending with feet together. Reverse directions for the repeat.

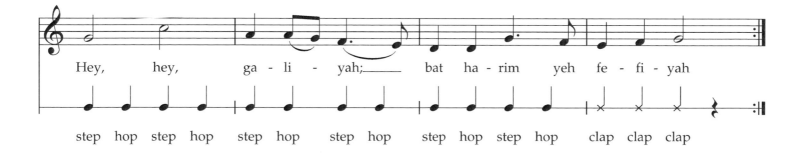

Moving towards the center of the circle in quarter note pulse, six step-hop patterns are followed by three hand claps in the air. Move backward on the repeat ending again with three hand claps.

A free translation of the text:

Put your hand in mine,
I am yours and you are mine
Hey, Galiyah, a beautiful daughter of the mountains

11. Jeremiah

Steven Calantropio

The exploration of scales that do not fall into traditional patterns opens ears to the sonorities of contemporary music. This exercise uses a *synthetic* pentatonic scale of such construction. Underlying the exercise is the idea of improvisation over a *ground bass;* one of the traditional developmental forms found in elemental music.

1. To begin, students prepare the barred instruments by removing the G and A bars, replacing F with F♯ and B with B♭.

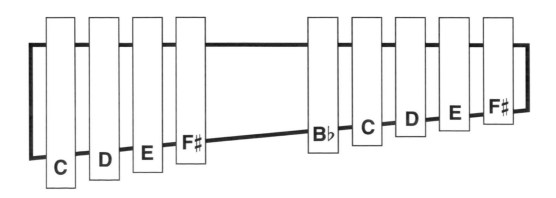

Then, ask students to repeat the traditional rhyme:

"Jeremiah, blow the fire, puff, puff, puff. First you blow it gently, then you blow it rough!"

Students explore the text by speaking the poem in various rhythms. Finally, arrive at the following rhythm which will serve as the basis for the rest of the lesson development:

Jer-e-mi- ah, blow the fi- re, Puff, puff, puff, First you blow it gent- ly, Then you blow it rough!

When students are familiar with this version, ask them to listen to you speak the text in rhythm while they step, alternating feet each time they sense a rest. They should step six times. Encourage students to attempt to step the six footsteps while speaking and eventually clapping the rhythm of the text.

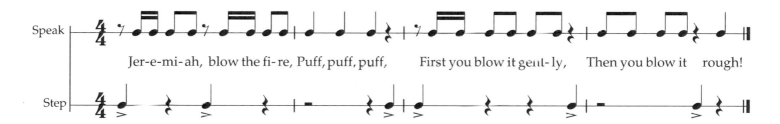

2. Now students can move to barred instruments. As you speak the poem, ask them to play the six foot steps as a series of pitches starting on low C and ending on high C. This pattern becomes a *ground bass*; a concept that can later be discussed with students with regard to its historical context. Assign this part to bass xylophones with the direction that it is an ostinato and must be played continually throughout the exercise.

3. Now, students echo the following rhythm through body percussion. Transfer this pattern to alto xylophones on pitches indicated in the score. Students listen to the bass and alto xylophone parts played together.

4. Begin to teach the melody phrase by phrase. The intervals in the synthetic scale make it difficult to sing but easy to play. Speak the first word **Je-re-mi-ah** asking

the students to begin on high E and play a four note stepwise descending pattern with this rhythm. The next phrase **blow the fi-re** moves in sequence down one bar, starting on D. In this way, aurally dictate each set of words giving the starting pitch and the melodic curve until the melody is secure on soprano xylophones. You may want the soprano xylophones to use hard mallets to accentuate the percussive qualities of the melody.

5. The suspended cymbal should be sounded on the first beat of the theme but not on the repeat. It serves as an aural marker for the improvisation to follow. After playing the melody, ostinato, and bass twice, eliminate the melody from the setting and allow students to improvise over the bass and alto xylophone accompaniment for two repetitions of the bass pattern before returning to the starting theme. We have created a *rondo* form with improvisatory episodes. **(A–B–A–C–A etc.)**. The cymbal marks the start of each improvisation and each return to the **A** theme. Encourage improvisations on barred and unpitched percussion instruments that reflect the fresh percussive and tonal effects of the theme. Suggest repeated accented tones, dissonances, glissandi and new ways to produce sounds from the instrument such as using the ribbed edge of the mallet handle in a scraping motion against the edge of a bar.

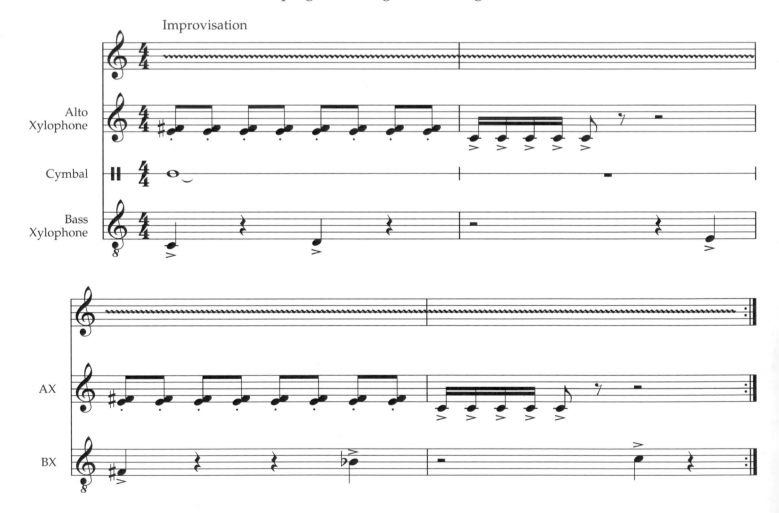

An introduction can be cumulatively developed starting with the ground bass, adding the alto xylophone. Use the reverse, fading away, for a coda.

12. Sing Hallelujah

Steven Calantropio

D.C. al Fine

As students progress, leaving the realm of elemental music making to enter more traditional performance and compositional approaches, creative process teaching techniques continue to have great value for the teacher. Such techniques can bring the participant to an understanding of the underlying harmonies and rhythms of *Sing Hallelujah*. Once these underlying patterns are explored, written notation has more meaning to the singers because they have developed an understanding of the underlying elements of the work.

1. Students observe and echo the following word patterns, realizing that throughout this exercise, the eighth note remains constant:

Mat - thew   Chris-to-pher   Mar - y El - len

Try aurally dictating combinations of these patterns to create longer rhythms, asking students to speak and/or clap the resulting rhythms. Eventually, direct students' attention to the pattern noted here. Students clap the pattern, repeating it.

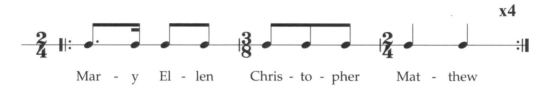

Mar - y El - len   Chris - to - pher   Mat - thew

Some students can explore this rhythm in movement creating dance steps based on underlying metrical impulses of the pattern while others accompany on hand drums.

2. Invite students to observe the following notations of triads in G major. Divide students into three groups. While they observe the following notation, assign one group to sing the lowest note of each measure. Another group is assigned to the middle note and the third is assigned the top note. It will be necessary to point out the missing member of the V7 and final inverted I triad and to explain that such changes are sometimes made for the sake of voice leading. You may also want to employ the strategy for learning harmonic movement described in lesson 9, p. 45 to strengthen the sense of harmonic changes.

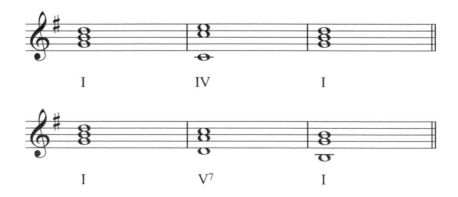

I   IV   I

I   V⁷   I

58

When students can securely sing each line formed by the members of the triad, they are ready to sing these parts with the rhythm learned previously:

Mar - y - el - len   Chris-to-pher   Mat - thew   Mar - y - el - len   Chris-to-pher   Mat - thew

Now substitute the text of the *Sing Hallelujah.*

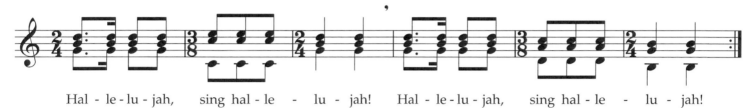

Hal - le-lu - jah,   sing hal - le   -   lu - jah!   Hal - le-lu - jah,   sing hal - le   -   lu - jah!

Students now can begin to adapt their preparatory exercises in rhythm and harmony to the actual arrangement of the **A** section. A performance of *Sing Hallelujah* can include movement based on the preparatory exercises, addition of unpitched percussion such as cymbals, or the playing of the three vocal parts on recorders. Additions to the score should reinforce the rhythmic, exultant nature of the piece.

The new elements in the **B** section of *Sing Hallelujah* challenge the teacher to continue using effective process teaching techniques. In your exploration of the pieces and processes presented in this book, you will have gained facility with many effective process teaching tools. You may find that your skills with process teaching techniques can provide solutions to the musical problems these few measures of the **B** section seem to pose.

Here are some tips to get you started.

- Can you find different speech patterns to teach the new rhythms of each voice part, perhaps again based on smaller rhythmic units such as names?
- Can movement activities be developed that would help students feel the new metric changes?
- Are there repetitive structural phrase units in each voice part that will assist in learning the entire B section?
- Do you have a new teaching tool that you can employ that will help in this teachingto explore this material?

As your students grow in their understanding of the elements and functions of music, you will also grow in the depth of your understanding of the teaching techniques that will bring elemental music to life.

ABOUT THE AUTHOR

Steven Calantropio, recently retired, taught public school music in River Edge, New Jersey for 31 years. During that time he has become a well-known clinician and workshop presenter both nationally and internationally. Educated at New Jersey's William Paterson University, Ohio University, the Manhattan School of Music and the Orff Institute in Salzburg, Austria, Mr. Calantropio continues to compose, arrange, teach and write about music education. He lives in the small town of Hamburg, in scenic northern New Jersey's Sussex County.